Active
Play times

Active Playtimes

Over 70 playground activities for fit,
healthy and happy kids

Roger Hurn

A & C Black • London

Published in 2006 by A & C Black Publishers Ltd
38 Soho Square, London W1D 3HB
www.acblack.com

ISBN-10: 0 7136 7724 4
ISBN-13: 978 0 7136 7724 9

A CIP record for this book is available from the British Library.

Note: While every effort has been made to ensure that the content of this book is as technically accurate and as sound as possible, neither the author nor the publisher can accept responsibility for any injury or loss sustained as a result of the use of this material.

A & C Black uses paper produced with elemental chlorine-free pulp, harvested from managed sustainable forests.

Acknowledgements
Cover and inside illustrations by Jan Smith
Inside design by Fiona Grant

Typeset by Palimpsest Book Production Ltd
Grangemouth, Stirlingshire

Printed and bound in Great Britain by Caligraving Ltd, Thetford, Norfolk.

Contents

This book is dedicated to all the children, helpers and teachers who've shared their playground games with me over the years, and to Rachel Hooper for her enthusiastic help and advice.

Introduction

Take a look around any school playground and you'll notice a worrying sight – children are becoming more and more overweight. The NHS's health and social care information centre has found that one in three 11–15-year-olds are overweight or obese, which can have serious consequences for their health. In fact, according to a national survey conducted by the British Paediatric Surveillance Unit at Bristol University in 2005, there are signs that obesity-related diabetes in children in the UK may be heading for the kind of epidemic proportions seen in the United States. In 2004, child health workers discovered at least 83 children who had been diagnosed with type 2 diabetes brought on by obesity. Type 2 diabetes is a condition caused mainly by lifestyle choices and used to be found only in middle-aged or elderly adults; indeed, up until relatively recently it was unheard of in British children. As the long-term effects of diabetes can include blindness, amputation, kidney disease, heart conditions and strokes, many of our children are facing a very bleak future unless we, as teachers, help them to do something about it now.

Of course, it is easy to shrug one's shoulders and say that it is society as a whole that is to blame; that parents should take more responsibility for what their children eat or that the government should legislate to ban adverts promoting junk food. This may be true, but it doesn't help us address the issue of what we can do to help children lead healthier lifestyles.

The celebrity chef Jamie Oliver has received widespread praise for his crusade to persuade the powers that be to introduce better quality food into school kitchens. Of course, raising awareness of nutritional issues and giving children the option of choosing low-fat meals is very laudable, but it's only one part of the equation. Eating sensibly will not reduce children's weight and improve their health unless it is linked to a programme of exercise.

We all know that the curriculum is already bursting at the seams and there is no room to shoehorn yet another lot of activities into it. However, as teachers, we cannot stand idly by while the problem of childhood obesity gets steadily worse. So, what is the solution? Well, we need to think of ways to integrate exercise into daily school life without it placing an impossible burden on the curriculum. There is really only one way to do this: by taking advantage of the opportunities offered by playtimes to get children fit and active. *Active Playtimes* gives teachers a blueprint for doing exactly that. This book will show you how to:

- reflect on what is happening currently at playtimes in your school
- organise playtimes productively
- include all children
- train colleagues and helpers
- improve children's fitness
- improve children's motivation
- improve children's ability to cooperate
- reduce the incidence of bullying
- promote positive ethnic awareness by introducing a wide range of games from around the world
- meet health and safety requirements
- evaluate whether educational objectives for playtimes are being met
- make playtimes fun.

Healthy children are happy children and healthy, happy children are much more likely to be alert and attentive in class – which can only be good for their academic development. So, all things considered, can you or the children you teach really afford to be without this book?

PART 1

Implementing an active playtimes policy

1 What's going on?

Each school is unique, but there are certain trends that affect all schools. For instance, have you ever walked across the playground and seen that nearly every child is suddenly playing with the same type of new toy? If you picked up the phone in the office and called up schools across the country, chances are they'd all report the same phenomenon. It's as if there's a 'craze-maker' who sits in a vast warehouse hidden inside the crater of an extinct volcano and telepathically instructs children everywhere to purchase and play with the same toys at exactly the same time. In recent years there have been crazes for Top Trumps, Pokemon, yo-yos, Beanie Babies, cyber pets and Beyblades, to name just a few. Although the craze-maker is fictitious and the latest childhood fads are usually benign, the trend towards childhood obesity isn't. However, as I said in the introduction, you can buck this particular trend by using the playground in the way it was always meant to be used – for playing games.

The steps you have to take on the road to reaching your goal need to be carefully thought through and planned if they are to be effective; this can only be achieved by thinking strategically.

Strategic thinking

We live in an age of sound bites and quick-fix solutions whereby someone – usually an irascible newspaper columnist – notices that something is not as it should be and thunders on about it. Politicians get in a flap and promise action, which often amounts to little more than a few attention-grabbing headlines and lots of clichéd rhetoric, usually containing the words 'education' and 'shake-up'. Blame for the situation is duly apportioned to the usual suspects and then, before anything of substance is done to address the problem, the whole thing is brushed aside by the next moral panic. Only rarely does someone actually think strategically about what needs to be done and then put those thoughts into action.

Of course, you can't influence anything on a national scale, but you can make a significant difference to what is happening in your school by thinking and acting strategically about how to help your pupils become fitter and healthier. The process of thinking strategically works like this:

1. Analyse a given situation.
2. Identify the problem or problems arising from that situation.
3. Communicate effectively and persuasively with key members of staff.
4. Generate a proposed solution or solutions.
5. Anticipate the impact of applying the proposed solutions.
6. Decide which is the most appropriate solution to apply.
7. Apply the solution.
8. Evaluate the outcomes.
9. Make appropriate adjustments.

This may sound quite complex, but it actually isn't. This can be demonstrated by applying the process of thinking strategically to a very simple situation – it's late at night and your stomach's rumbling (see figure 1.1).

FIGURE 1.1 STRATEGIC THINKING

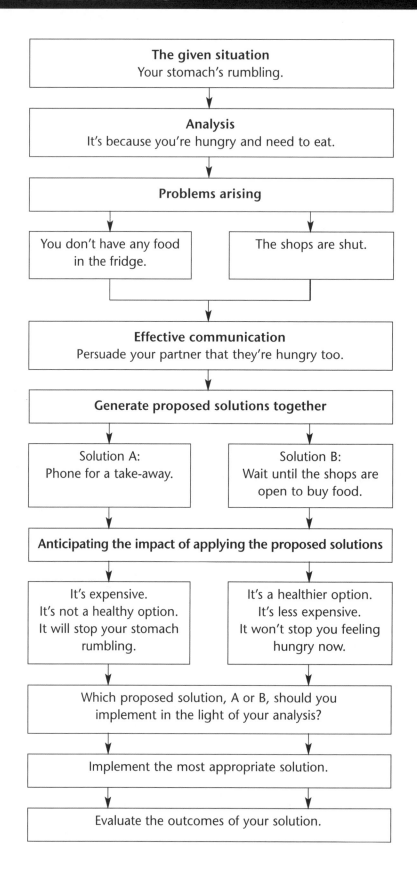

Of course, addressing how your school can tackle the problem of children's lack of fitness by using playtimes more effectively is far more complicated than deciding whether or not to order a late-night take-away, but the principles of strategic thinking apply equally in both cases. By utilising them, you and the rest of the staff can make a considered judgement about what is likely to be the most effective and appropriate solution. You can also apply this model to every problem you encounter in your efforts to establish active playtimes, such as training playtime supervisors and so on. However, you need to remember that each option you consider will have implications and consequences, both intended and unintended; the beauty of strategic thinking is that it allows you to anticipate what these are likely to be, and to factor them into your calculations, before you commit yourself to a particular course of action.

Moreover, although we all try to be objective, children's health is an emotive issue and people will inevitably inject their own subjective views into the equation. For instance, some staff members may be sensitive about their own lack of fitness or excessive weight, while others may talk disapprovingly about 'fitness fanaticism'. One or two may even think it isn't part of their job to worry about what the children do during breaktimes. This is where you'll need to bring a measure of pragmatism to the process and be at your most persuasive if you're going to arrive at a range of solutions that everyone can agree on and will implement.

Once you've discussed all your options, made decisions based on the evidence and embarked on your chosen course of action, you'll need to evaluate your progress on a regular basis and adjust or fine-tune your actions accordingly to make sure you remain on track to securing your goal. The following Strategic Thinking Chart (figure 1.2) will be useful in helping you and your colleagues to focus your thoughts as you progress towards your ultimate goal of making the children fitter, healthier and happier through playground activities.

FIGURE 1.2 STRATEGIC THINKING CHART

Goal: To help the children become fitter and more active.	
What is the current situation in our school?	
Why is this? What are the implications?	
Who can help change this situation?	
How can we change this situation?	
What are the likely outcomes (intended/ unintended) of the proposed solutions?	
What course of action shall we implement?	
How successful have we been in achieving our goal?	
What adjustments or fine-tuning do we need to make?	

KEY POINTS

● British children are becoming more obese.

● This has serious implications for their health.

● Teachers can use playtimes to help children get fitter.

● Strategic thinking is a useful process for generating solutions to problems as it anticipates the outcomes of each course of action and allows for considered decision-making.

● Regular evaluation of progress helps keep projects on track.

2 Gathering information

If it is to have any chance of succeeding, your strategy for helping your pupils become fitter and healthier must be based on an objective analysis of the situation as it exists in your school. However, how can you be sure of what exactly that situation is?

How fit are the children in your school?

Everyone will be implementing the PE curriculum during lesson times, so you and your colleagues could use PE lessons to check children's basic levels of fitness by giving them some simple age-appropriate tasks to do, such as:

- How many star jumps can you do in 60 seconds?
- How quickly can you run 50 metres?
- How many step-ups can you do in 60 seconds?
- How many times can you bounce on the spot in 60 seconds?
- How many times can you skip over a rope in 60 seconds?
- How many 10-metre shuttle runs can you do in 60 seconds?
- How many wall press-ups can you do in 60 seconds?
- How many squat thrusts can you do in 60 seconds?

and so on.

By recording and dating each child's performance, you will have something against which to measure the improvement in their fitness after you have instigated the proposed active playtimes programme.

However, the government's view that two hours of physical activity a week, including the National Curriculum for physical education and extra-curricular activities, should be an aspiration for all schools is hardly likely to be enough to reverse the accelerating trend towards childhood obesity. Therefore, you also need to check if the playground is being used to maximum effect during breaktimes.

How is the playground being used at playtimes?

The only reliable way of finding out how the playground is actually used at playtimes is to conduct an audit. Decide what questions you need answers to, such as:

- Is there provision for children to play games other than mass football matches?
- Are children standing around looking bored rather than playing?
- Why is it that so many children try to sneak back into school during playtimes?
- Is there any evidence that the children know how to play a variety of games?
- What kind of games are the children playing?

List all your questions and visit the playground at break and lunchtimes over a period of several days to observe what is going on. Figure 2.1 shows an example of a completed observation form.

FIGURE 2.1 COMPLETED OBSERVATION FORM

General observations of how the children used the playground during morning break.		Date: September 2006
Question	**Approximate percentage**	**Comments**
Approximately what percentage of the children were engaged in active play?	70%	The children were mainly engaged in chasing each other, skipping or playing with small balls.
Approximately what percentage of the children were engaged in mass team games, e.g. football, touch rugby, netball?	0%	Large team games are banned during morning playtime.
Approximately what percentage of the children were engaged in small group games, e.g. skipping, hopscotch, tag?	70%	Some girls from Year 3 were skipping. A mixed group from Year 6 were playing hopscotch. Some boys from Years 5 and 6 were playing 'squash' against the playground wall.
Approximately what percentage of children were isolated and/or inactive?	30%	A few children seemed to be wandering about or standing on their own. Most of the rest were standing around in small groups talking.
How competently were the children playing, e.g. was everyone equally involved; were some little more than bystanders; did they observe the rules?	N/A	Most of the chasing games seemed to be a bit inconclusive and kept petering out. The children playing hopscotch seemed more interested in posing and arguing than in playing properly. The children playing 'squash' were very involved but got cross when other children ran in front of them. The children skipping played happily.
Were there any organised activities for the children, e.g. traditional games?	N/A	Only the hopscotch.
Did the supervisors lead any of the children's games?	N/A	No. The teachers on duty chatted to each other.
Are there any play leaders (either adults or older pupils) involved with playground activities?	N/A	No.

Active Playtimes: Key Stage 1+2 © Roger Hurn 2006, A & C Black Publishers Ltd

Questionnaires

You will also need to find out the opinions of those who use the playground, which includes both the children and the adults who supervise them. For example, do lots of children dread the time spent hanging around on what can only be described as a concrete wasteland? Do they actually know how to play games? Do those who supervise the playground have the knowledge, skills, ability and, most of all, the desire to do more than just patrol it clutching a mug of coffee or tea in their hands? In order to find out, you'll have to ask the children and adults to complete a simple, age-appropriate questionnaire with open-ended questions. This will ensure that you give everyone the chance to offer their thoughts, which will be vital when it comes to achieving a consensus on the need to change things for the better.

To ensure you get 100 per cent participation from the children, the whole staff will have to help you distribute the questionnaires and encourage the children to fill them in. In terms of organisation and clarity, it may be easier and more appropriate if, after class discussions, the teachers of the younger classes act as scribes to fill in the questionnaire with the children.

The forms on pages 16–19 can be used as templates. Here are some extracts from examples of completed questionnaires:

FIGURE 2.2 QUESTIONNAIRE FOR CHILDREN

What do YOU think of playtimes?

What do you like about morning playtime?	What don't you like about morning playtime?
I can talk to my friends after sitting quietly in assembly, which is boring.	It's too short to really do anything.

What would make morning playtime better?

It would be better if it was a bit longer. Sometimes assembly goes on and doesn't finish on time and so we don't have much time to play.

What do you like about lunch playtime?	What don't you like about lunch playtime?
Sometimes the supervisors play games with us.	The supervisors are mostly too busy stopping fights and telling people off to play games. The boys won't let girls play football and they take up all the playground.

What would make lunch playtime better?

The boys shouldn't be allowed to take up all the playground playing football. It would be better if we had some skipping ropes and hoops and stuff to play with. It would be good if the teachers taught us some games to play. That would give us something to do and it might stop some of the fighting. Also, if we knew some games we could teach them to the kids in the infants.

What do you like about afternoon playtime?	What don't you like about afternoon playtime?
We don't have to share the playground with the infants so that gives us more room to play.	We don't really have anything to do. Even the boys aren't allowed to play football.

What would make afternoon playtime better?

If we had some netball and basketball nets or some hopscotch markings on the playground.

   Active Playtimes: Key Stage 1+2 © Roger Hurn 2006, A & C Black Publishers Ltd

FIGURE 2.3 QUESTIONNAIRE FOR TEACHERS

What do you think of playtimes?

Do you think children are making the best use of playtimes?

No I don't. I think the behaviour is diabolical. All they seem to do is squabble with each other.

Why do you think this is?

They don't have any idea of how to play sensibly. They are really thoughtless and selfish, although the playground is a pretty boring place. I think they get fed up and take it out on each other.

What can we do to improve the situation?

It might be an idea to put down some playground markings – like hopscotch – and get the midday meal supervisors to teach them some games. We could even have some equipment like small balls, beanbags, skipping ropes and hoops for them to play with, although the supervisors would have to keep a close eye on how they used them.

What are the cost and training implications of your suggestions?

I don't suppose the beanbags and skipping ropes would be too expensive, but it might be difficult to train up the supervisors. Though I think it should be part of their job description to teach the children how to play games properly.

FIGURE 2.4 QUESTIONNAIRE FOR SUPERVISORS

What do you think of playtimes?

Do you think children are making the best use of playtimes?

Not really. Some of the children play together nicely but others seem to be more interested in arguing than playing. They're always saying they're bored. The little ones don't like it either because the older children knock them over when they're chasing around after footballs.

Why do you think this is?

I don't think anyone's ever taught them how to play properly. When I was their age I used to like skipping and we played lots of skipping games. But children today don't seem to know any of the old skipping rhymes. The only game they know is football and they don't even play that properly.

What can we do to improve the situation?

The teachers have got to teach them how to play without arguing with each other. I'd like to teach the children some of the skipping games I used to play but we haven't got any ropes and anyway I'm too busy sorting out squabbles.

What are the cost and training implications of your suggestions?

Skipping ropes don't cost much and I already know the skipping games. I think some of the other supervisors know some other games but we'd need more help on the playground if we're going to be playing games with groups of children instead of keeping them in order.

Even a cursory reading of the three example questionnaires shows that there are discrepancies between a child's, a teacher's and a supervisor's perception of playtimes, although none of them present a very positive view of the current situation. Certainly none of them offer any evidence that the children are getting much exercise at playtimes. However, all three have provided pointers to the way forward. They have also given you an insight into the attitudes each has towards playtimes.

The **child** has identified that the children look to both the supervisors *and* the teachers to help them play more productively. She has even indicated a willingness to learn new skills and pass them on to younger children.

The **teacher**, on the other hand, sees the children as being thoughtless and selfish and puts the responsibility for doing something about it onto the shoulders of the supervisors. However, the teacher does concede that the playground is lacking in amenities and that the supervisors will need training.

The **supervisor**, for her part, feels that the teachers should do more to change the children's attitudes. She is battling to keep things under control while lamenting the fact that children don't seem to know how to play the games that she did as a girl. She is aware of her skills in this area, but needs to be empowered to put them to good use.

Of course, these are only three possible responses out of many, but you can see how feedback like this provides you with the sort of understanding and insights that should inform the strategic thinking decision-making model we looked at in Chapter One (see pages 3–5).

A SWOT analysis

Once you've gathered and collated all the information from the staff and pupils at your school, your next task will be to analyse it. This can be done by using a SWOT analysis. You're probably well aware that all sorts of organisations employ SWOT analysis to highlight their **S**trengths, **W**eaknesses and **O**pportunities and to identify **T**hreats. However, you can also use the SWOT methodology to analyse the information you've collated.

In your school's case, where your objective is to find out what's really happening in regard to the children being active at playtimes, you can define strengths as the things your school is already doing well and doesn't need to change. Weaknesses can be identified as those things your school isn't doing well – or even not doing at all. Opportunities are things that your school can build on and develop, while threats are things that would be either very difficult or impossible to alter.

Let's examine what this might mean in practice. For example, it may be that there is a consensus among all the staff and children that there is less trouble on the playground when the lunchtime supervisors organise and play games with the children. This would constitute a strength. If, however, there is a consensus that football is dominating the playground to the detriment of the vast majority of children, this would constitute a weakness. Having identified the fact that lunch playtimes are more enjoyable when the supervisors play games with the children, you can then list 'developing the supervisors' skills in this area' as an opportunity to actively involve more children, although this opportunity may have to be tempered by the threat that any extra training for supervisors will have to be paid for out of the school's budget.

Figure 2.5 shows a simplified example of a completed SWOT analysis form.

FIGURE 2.5 A SWOT ANALYSIS OF THE VIEWS OF TEACHERS, SUPERVISORS AND CHILDREN ABOUT PLAYTIMES AT ELVIRIA PRIMARY SCHOOL

Strengths (What's working)	Weaknesses (What isn't working)
• Children like it when supervisors play games with them. • The supervisors like to teach the children games. • Some children enjoy playing ball games. • A few older children include younger children in their games, to the benefit of all.	• Many children don't play properly. • Football is dominating the playground. • Younger children feel intimidated. • Many children don't want to be out in the playground and would rather be inside. • Footballs are unsuitable for use in a crowded playground. • There are no playground markings for games. • Children don't have access to small games equipment. • Lots of children are bored at playtimes. • There is no playground apparatus for the children.
Opportunities (Things we can develop)	Threats (Things we can't change)
• We can train the supervisors so they are better able to organise games for the children at lunchtime. • We can limit the playground area in which football is played. • We can provide small games equipment for the children. • We can provide some playground apparatus. • The teachers can teach their classes playground games. • We can train older children to be play leaders.	• We don't have the budget to buy in extra playground supervisors.

When you've completed your SWOT analysis, communicate your findings to key members of staff. You and they will then be in a strong position to begin to generate possible solutions as to how you can make playtimes more productive, both in terms of combating the children's lack of fitness and in reaping the benefits that accrue when the children have been engaged in playing properly rather than arguing and fighting.

KEY POINTS

● An objective analysis of what's happening in your school at playtimes can only be undertaken after an audit has been conducted.

● In order for the audit to be accurate, everyone involved must be consulted.

● Observation sheets and questionnaires are effective methods of information gathering.

● Questionnaires should be open-ended and age-appropriate.

● A SWOT analysis (Strengths, Weaknesses, Opportunities, Threats) is an effective way of analysing the information collected.

FIGURE 2.6 OBSERVATIONS TEMPLATE

General observations of how the children used the playground during morning break.		Date:
Question	**Approximate percentage**	**Comments**
Approximately what percentage of the children were engaged in active play?		
Approximately what percentage of the children were engaged in mass team games, e.g. football, touch rugby, netball?		
Approximately what percentage of the children were engaged in small group games, e.g. skipping, hopscotch, tag?		
Approximately what percentage of the children were isolated and/or inactive?		
How competently were the children playing, e.g. was everyone equally involved; were some little more than bystanders; did they observe the rules?		
Were there any organised activities for the children, e.g. traditional games?		
Did the supervisors lead any of the children's games?		
Are there any play leaders (either adults or older pupils) involved with playground activities?		

FIGURE 2.7 QUESTIONNAIRE FOR CHILDREN – TEMPLATE

What do YOU think of playtimes?

What do you like about morning playtime?	What don't you like about morning playtime?

What would make morning playtime better?

What do you like about lunch playtime?	What don't you like about lunch playtime?

What would make lunch playtime better?

What do you like about afternoon playtime?	What don't you like about afternoon playtime?

What would make afternoon playtime better?

FIGURE 2.8 QUESTIONNAIRE FOR ADULTS – TEMPLATE

What do you think of playtimes?

Do you think children are making the best use of playtimes?

Why do you think this is?

What can we do to improve the situation?

What are the cost and training implications of your suggestions?

FIGURE 2.9 A SWOT ANALYSIS – TEMPLATE

Strengths (What's working)	Weaknesses (What isn't working)
Opportunities (Things we can develop)	**Threats** (Things we can't change)

3 The way forward

When you and your colleagues have discussed the results from the surveys and questionnaires and looked at the SWOT analysis in detail, you will have all the information you need to generate a solution to the problem of how to improve the fitness of the children in your school through playground activities. However, before you do so, it will help you to convince doubters, as well as focus your minds, if you and your colleagues hold a 'thought shower' session to highlight the advantages of having active playtimes and why play is so important to children. The following pages are intended to offer some ideas to inform your discussions.

The importance of play

The famous child psychologist Dr Benjamin Spock once said that play is the work of children. This is an acute observation because when they play children are trying out new ideas, creating sense and order in the world, learning how to include others, learning how to make decisions, learning how to problem-solve, learning how to lose with good grace as well as how to win, learning to compromise and using their imaginations – as well as getting much-needed exercise. But how do active playtimes contribute to this?

Active playtimes reduce incidences of bullying

Research has shown that children who are fully involved in playing are less likely to become bullies, as communal games help children to play together and to communicate more during play (Blatchford, 1998). By playing structured games, children have the opportunity to recognise each other's strengths as well as to learn how to resolve potential conflicts through the application of universally agreed rules.

Active playtimes provide the opportunity to teach children to be more cooperative by playing games together

Activities such as hopscotch or skipping games promote interaction. Children have to talk to each other and cooperate in order to play them properly and, by engaging in this process, children learn how to work together.

Active playtimes help to develop children's thinking skills

In order to play games successfully, children need to be able to understand and apply tactics and strategies in flexible and creative ways. For example, if children are playing a simple game of Bucket Ball (see page 81), they will have to decide whether to defend their bucket zonally or by marking player for player. Each strategy has its merits, but neither one is appropriate in all cases. Therefore, the children will have to learn how to assess a situation quickly and adapt their tactics accordingly.

Active playtimes reduce the number of squabbles

All teachers know that an awful lot of curriculum time can be wasted in trying to sort out squabbles that started at breaktime. One way to find out exactly how much time is wasted is for each class teacher to keep a log and record the amount of time they spend on resolving these arguments. The results are instructive, though nearly always depressing. However, if children are involved in enough exciting games and activities at playtime, they are far less likely to become so involved in conflict.

 Active Playtimes: Key Stage 1+2 © Roger Hurn 2006, A & C Black Publishers Ltd

Active playtimes give the opportunity to involve older children as play leaders/play friends

There is an old proverb that says, 'If you want to help a child, let them help someone else'. This is excellent advice. Recruiting older children to work with younger children raises their self-esteem and helps foster integration and social inclusion across the school community. The older children have a chance to develop both a sense of responsibility and their leadership skills in a way that complements and supports the work of teachers and playground supervisors.

Active playtimes are more fun for everyone

Nobody enjoys feeling bored or lonely any more than children want to be bullied or adults want to spend their time intervening in quarrels. A well-ordered and structured playtime with adequate and appropriate resources, where everyone knows what is expected of them and where they can join in with lots of interesting and exciting games, is the perfect antidote to this.

Skills and resources audit

When you've held your thought shower session and come up with ideas on how to implement active playtimes, refer back to the strategic thinking model discussed in Chapter One (see pages 3–5). You'll see that this is the point at which you assess the risks, implications and possible outcomes of the various courses of action you're proposing. To do this you'll need to conduct a skills and resources audit to see if you have the expertise and equipment necessary to deliver these solutions. For an example of a skills and resources audit, see figure 3.1.

FIGURE 3.1 SAMPLE SKILLS AND RESOURCES AUDIT				
Proposal	Current staff skills, expertise, resources	Possible options	Cost implications	Time scale
To teach the children a selection of traditional playground games.	PE coordinator organises twilight INSET sessions to teach the staff games.	Class teachers teach games in PE lessons.	Cost of book of traditional playground games.	First twilight session after half term. All games taught to children by end of term.

As a result of your audit, you may have to either supplement your skills and resources or modify your solutions in the light of what you have available or can afford in terms of time and money.

A resources and skills audit template can be found on page 26.

Setting targets

When you've collected information, analysed the situation, generated solutions, assessed the implications and decided on a course of action, you will be in a position to set targets for the implementation of your plan. These targets should be SMART: Specific, Measurable, Achievable, Realistic and Time-framed. In practice, this means:

- If the targets are too wide and involved to be achieved in a reasonable period of time, it's unlikely that they will ever be realised.
- If they are too abstract, they will be impossible to measure.
- If they are too complex to be easily understood, they won't be achievable.
- If they make impossible demands on resources, they're unrealistic.
- If targets are to be achieved, you need to set deadlines so everyone knows when they should be completed. Deadlines also mean that progress will be reviewed at regular intervals.

Your targets could range from the very simple, such as finding a collection of playground games for the children to play, to the more complex, such as instituting a training programme to show lunchtime supervisors how to organise and deliver a programme of structured playground activities designed to raise children's fitness levels. However, it cannot be stressed enough that everyone involved must have a voice in deciding these targets.

Drawing up an action plan

When you and your colleagues have defined your goals and agreed your targets, you will be in a position to put together an action plan that makes explicit:

- what is going to be done
- who is going to be responsible for doing it
- when they're going to do it
- how they're going to do it
- where they're going to do it
- how much it's all going to cost

Having an action plan ensures clarity of purpose and accountability and acts as a spur to actually getting things done. For an example of an action plan, see figure 3.2.

FIGURE 3.2 SAMPLE ACTION PLAN				
Description of proposed action	Person/s responsible	Schedule	Cost	Deadline
Recruiting and training play leaders.	Year 6 class teachers.	Select appropriate children. Teachers to work with them to enable them to work safely and responsibly with younger children at lunchtimes. Provide opportunities for the older pupils to learn leadership skills, how to play team games with younger children and how to organise structured play activities in an appropriate environment. Support play leaders in the delivery of lunchtime sessions where they can practise the skills they have learned in teaching younger pupils to cooperate with each other in a safe and caring environment.	None.	Autumn Half Term.

Success criteria

You must also be able to evaluate whether or not you are on track to achieving your stated goals. This is where success criteria come into their own. Your targets will have set you on the road to where you want to go, but you won't know when you've arrived unless you have a clear idea of how to recognise the place when you get there. For example, if your goal is to find an appropriate collection of playground games at a cost of £20 or less in time for the start of the Spring Term, your success criteria will only be achieved when and if you manage to buy a suitable book within the budget and by the set date (see figure 3.3).

FIGURE 3.3 SUCCESS CRITERIA						
Description of proposed action	Person/s responsible	Schedule	Cost	Deadline	Success criteria	Outcome
Finding an appropriate collection of play-ground games.	PE coordinator.	Research on internet, bookshops, publishers' catalogues.	£20	Start of Spring Term.	Finding and buying an appropriate book, within the budget, by the start of the Spring Term.	

Therefore, no action plan is complete without containing agreed success criteria. As with the targets in your plan, your success criteria should be measurable, realistic and finite, otherwise they won't be achievable.

A resources and skills audit template can be found on page 26.

A word of warning

Having an action plan is no guarantee that you will achieve your goal of making the children in your school fitter through active playtimes. The changes you want to implement will only succeed in the long term if everyone is committed not only to making them happen, but also to sustaining them. Indeed, all projects, whether they are grandiose or simple, are prey to the same glitches, snags and pitfalls. Your efforts to improve children's fitness through playground activities will be no exception. However, problems can be avoided by ensuring that:

- everyone concerned has agreed and understands what is to be achieved
- the necessary resources are provided as agreed and when required
- everyone keeps to the time schedules in the action plan; if this is not the case, the schedules must be re-assessed immediately otherwise the project will drift
- the project has the full and active backing of the senior management team.

To recap

At this point in the proceedings it makes sense to summarise everything you'll need to do if you are going to establish active playtimes in your school. The following *aide-memoire* is intended to serve precisely that purpose.

- Be clear as to your rationale.
- Assess the current situation.
- Collect evidence and opinion.
- Analyse the information gathered.
- Secure the agreement of the whole staff on the need for the children to be fitter.

- Work together with the whole staff to decide the most effective ways to implement active playtimes.
- Draw up an action plan with built-in success criteria.
- Start the process of implementation.
- Evaluate progress and adjust actions accordingly.

KEY POINTS

- Play is extremely important to a child's physical, social, emotional and cognitive development.

- In order to assess the risks, implications and possible outcomes of the various courses of action you're proposing, you'll need to conduct a skills and resources audit to see if you have the expertise and equipment necessary to achieve your aims.

- All targets should be SMART (Specific, Measurable, Achievable, Realistic, Time-framed).

- Your action plan should make explicit who, what, where, when and how you will achieve your targets.

- Success criteria help you to evaluate whether or not you have achieved your goals.

- Successful projects are those where everyone understands and shares the same goals; has adequate resources; keeps to the agreed schedule; and has the support of senior managers.

FIGURE 3.4 RESOURCES AND SKILLS AUDIT TEMPLATE					
Proposal	Current staff skills, expertise, resources	Possible options	Cost implications	Time scale	Decision

FIGURE 3.5 ACTION PLAN TEMPLATE						
Description of proposed action	Person/s responsible	Schedule	Cost	Deadline	Success Criteria	Outcome

4 Training

Now that you've completed the processes outlined so far in this book you will be well on your way to achieving the goal of having active playtimes in your school. However, you will almost certainly have realised that, if your school's policy is to succeed, you will have to get to grips with some training issues. It's a sad fact of life that in this 21st century world of X-boxes and PlayStations, many traditional games have been forgotten. Therefore, teachers, children and playground supervisors will all need help and advice on what games to play and how to play them, which means organising INSET sessions.

Lunchtime supervisors

Let's start by looking at lunchtime supervisors. The lunch break is the longest of the playtimes and is usually the one that creates the most difficulties in terms of the children's behaviour. It also makes it the most suitable for the purposes of helping children get fit. However, some teachers are understandably reluctant to get involved in managing the children during this time, so the responsibility usually falls squarely on the shoulders of the supervisors. It therefore makes sense to include them from the start in any plans for improving the quality of playtimes. The supervisors will have skills and knowledge that can make a vital contribution to the success of the active playtimes policy, but they must feel that they are a valued and integral part of the proposed changes. Otherwise, they could see the new policy as an implied criticism of their current efforts and not embrace your innovations wholeheartedly (see also 'A word of warning' on page 24).

However, even if the lunchtime supervisors have been on board from the start, it still makes sense to provide a separate training session or sessions especially for them as they will be bearing the brunt of this initiative. This will have some time and cost implications, but is essential to ensure their support and motivation. Your action plan for lunchtime supervisor training might look like figure 4.1.

FIGURE 4.1 SAMPLE ACTION PLAN FOR TRAINING LUNCHTIME SUPERVISORS						
Description of proposed action	Person/s responsible	Possible options	Cost implications	Time scale	Success Criteria	Outcome
To train lunchtime supervisors so that they can lead playground games sessions with the children.	PE coordinator, assistant head teacher, senior lunchtime supervisor.	These sessions can be done in the hall one hour before lunchtime.	Each supervisor will be paid to attend the INSET sessions. Total cost: £XXX.	All training sessions to be completed by Autumn Half Term.	All supervisors will understand the 'Active Playtimes' policy; what their role is; how they will work; and have knowledge of a range of playground games.	

Following are some sample INSET sessions for lunchtime supervisors.

Session 1

Aims

- To make the lunchtime supervisors aware of the need to institute a programme of active playtimes.

- To find out their thoughts and ideas on how an active playtime policy can be implemented at lunchtime.

- To assess their skills and training needs

Content

Begin by explaining why the school is adopting a policy of active playtimes, with its emphasis on improving the children's fitness. Give the supervisors an overview of what you have done so far and distribute the playtime questionnaire for them to complete (see page 12 for the template). Allow them enough time to fill it in and then invite their comments, questions and suggestions. Write these up on a flip chart.

Now ask the supervisors to suggest ways in which they might organise the lunch break to accommodate the new approach. Encourage them to assess the implications, both positive and negative, of each suggestion. For example, they may like the idea of playing and teaching the children games, but they may not be confident enough or have the knowledge to do so.

End the session by summarising the discussion and by securing agreement on what has been decided and what the next step will be.

Session 2

Aims

- To increase the supervisors' knowledge of playground games and how to play them.

- To give the supervisors some ideas of how to organise the games.

- To give the supervisors a sense of ownership of the activities.

Content

Start Session 2 by recapping on the previous session and give feedback on the information you gathered from the questionnaires. Next, address the training needs identified in the first session. For example, if the supervisors want more information about playground games and how to play them, you can begin by asking them to tell you about games that they liked and played when they were children or that they've seen being played elsewhere and think that the children in your school would enjoy. Make a note of how these games are played and then ask the supervisors to demonstrate some of the games to each other. In this way you can start to build up a collection of games that draws on the supervisors' own knowledge and strengths, which will increase their sense of ownership of the changes. Point out that the class teachers will be teaching these games during PE lessons, which will help the supervisors when they attempt to play them with the children.

The PE coordinator can demonstrate some simple games and show how they can be taught to groups of children. Give some practical advice on how to manage the children, such as:

- only play games that you know and are confident in teaching
- make your behavioural expectations for the games session clear and stick to them
- don't start with a huge group; build up numbers slowly
- make the rules clear at the start of the game
- make sure you have the resources (balls, bats, ropes and so on) needed to play the games
- don't be afraid to let the children see you're enjoying the games too
- give lots of vocal encouragement and praise
- keep the games short and leave the children wanting more.

Conclude the session by discussing how you will write up the games and keep them in such a way that they are accessible to everyone. For instance, you might decide to keep them in an 'Active Playtime Games' folder in the school office. Point out that it is intended that the 'Active Playtime Games Collection' will consist of games contributed by the whole school community, so it will be continually updated and improved.

You may want to hold a third INSET session for the supervisors, like the one outlined below, on how they can include children who are not gregarious or who find the idea of joining in with games intimidating.

Session 3

Aim

- To give lunchtime supervisors strategies to include all children in the active playtime games.

Content

Explain that some children who perceive themselves as uncoordinated, lacking in fitness or who

Active Playtimes: Key Stage 1+2 © Roger Hurn 2006, A & C Black Publishers Ltd

have low self-esteem may initially be reluctant to join in with playground games. Make it clear that children may also allow gender stereotyping to influence their reactions to certain activities. For example, at primary school girls are often more coordinated than boys and are at least their equals in terms of physical development, yet it is usually the boys who dominate the playground by engaging in physical activities like football while the girls can be relegated to the role of passive bystanders. Point out how this needn't be the case, but that it takes a concerted effort on the part of all concerned to challenge the ingrained attitudes and negative perceptions of both children and adults.

Discuss together how gender expectations and the language we use impact on the children and how, by altering the way we think, act and speak, we can have a huge influence on creating an inclusive or exclusive environment. Encourage the supervisors to examine their own expectations and language use and explore how, through adopting an inclusive approach, they can be proactive in involving all children in the games. List the suggestions and ideas on a flip chart.

Now show the supervisors that another very effective strategy for promoting inclusion is playing cooperative, rather than competitive, games. These take the pressure off children who are vulnerable or reluctant to join in by removing the 'I win – you lose' ethos and emphasising instead the notion of teamwork and tackling a challenge together. You can play some non-competitive games such as Amoebas or Shake-a-Hand (see Chapter 8) with the supervisors so they can see not only that non-competitive games can be active and fun, but also how they can use them with the children.

End the session by restating what you have all agreed about the inclusion strategies.

The teaching staff

The teaching staff will have been involved in the step-by-step process of the active playtimes initiative, but they will still benefit from a practical session that introduces them to the type of games the children will be playing.

Training session for teachers

Aims

- To secure the staff's commitment to teaching their classes the games in PE lessons.

- To teach the staff some of the games the children will be playing during their active playtimes.

- To get the staff to contribute games to the 'Active Playtime Games Collection'.

Content

Remind the staff why it's so important to help the children become fitter through active playtimes. Explain that, although the lunchtime supervisors will be leading game-playing sessions, it will make their job easier and be beneficial for the children if the staff set aside part of their PE time for teaching the children the games in the 'Active Playtime Games Collection'. When you've secured their agreement to do this, ask them for suggestions of games to teach the children. List them under various headings, for example non-competitive games, skipping games, chasing games, ball games and so on.

Next, ask the staff who came up with the most interesting or suitable games to demonstrate how to play them. You can divide the staff into groups and let them play some of the games in this book. Hopefully, they'll all have fun, which will reinforce their enthusiasm for the policy.

The last part of the INSET session can be spent with the staff deciding together which of the games they will teach to their classes.

Play leaders

Many schools that have embraced the idea of active playtimes have found it very rewarding to have children as play leaders. To mark their special status these play leaders can wear coloured PE bibs, sashes, jackets, hats or customised T-shirts so the other children know who they are. By involving the children as play leaders during active playtimes, you will give them an opportunity to develop their:

- leadership skills
- communication skills
- social skills
- confidence
- self-esteem
- empathy

However, it's not enough just to select some enthusiastic children, hand them the play leader T-shirts and expect them to be able to cope. They will need to be shown how to play, and also how to teach other children, a range of activities and games. They will also need clear, straightforward advice on how to:

- communicate effectively
- handle disputes and conflict
- be fair and even-handed
- work alongside the teachers and playground supervisors to complement what they are doing.

You will need several sessions to do this properly, but following are some suggestions for how you might work with a group of potential play leaders.

Session 1: Improving communication
Aim
- To improve the children's ability to communicate with other children.

Content
Put the children in pairs and ask them to think of the different ways the adults in the school use to get children's attention. When they have done this, ask them to share their ideas with the group as a whole. Write these ideas up on a flip chart, separating the strategies into positive in one column and negative in another. Have a discussion about why you've put some strategies in the negative column. Highlight why positive strategies such as simple gestures like putting fingers to the lips, positive body language, expectant facial expressions and using the children's names are likely to be more effective as a means of gaining children's attention. Discuss why shouting or issuing threats are very unlikely to lead to a successful outcome.

Session 2: Active listening

Aim

- To make the children realise that in order to mediate successfully in any dispute over alleged rule-breaking, they need to listen actively.

Content

Explain to the children that when they are leading games sessions there will be times when some children will break or bend the rules and arguments will occur. Ask them to suggest ways of dealing with this. Write their answers up on a flip chart and discuss their suggestions. Introduce them to the principles of active listening: being attentive to the speaker, not getting emotional, not interrupting them, and, when the speaker has made their point, restating it so the speaker knows they have been understood.

Explain that when people argue they often don't actually listen to what the other person is saying. They are too busy trying to make their own point. They contradict each other and deny the other person's description of a situation. Instead of thinking about what's best for everyone, they're trying to win the argument and get their own way. Point out to the play leaders that they can't behave like this as it's their job to be even-handed and apply the rules fairly. Reassure them that you know this isn't an easy thing to do, but tell them that active listening can help as it's a way of listening and responding to another person that improves mutual understanding. If the children all know that the play leaders are prepared to listen carefully without favouring one side or the other, the chances of the play leaders being able to develop a solution to the problem of rule breaking and the conflict it causes become much greater.

Give the play leaders some tips on the appropriate body language to adopt when listening actively: face the person with an open posture, lean slightly towards the speaker, maintain eye contact and try to stay calm and relaxed. Demonstrate what you mean, then role-play with the play leaders some examples of the conflict situations they might have to face and get them to apply and practise the skills of active listening.

Session 3: Working alongside teachers and supervisors

N.B. It would be very helpful if the senior lunchtime supervisor could attend this session.

Aim

- To show play leaders how to complement the work of teachers and supervisors during active playtimes.

Content

Explain to the play leaders that their job is to support the teachers and supervisors by helping the children play games with each other during breaktimes. Ask them to suggest how they can do this. List their answers on a flip chart and discuss them. Ideally, the answers will include:

- knowing how the active playtimes are structured and organised
- having a sound knowledge of a wide range of games and how to play them
- knowing where any required equipment is kept and having it ready and available at the right time
- understanding that they are responsible for collecting and returning any equipment, such as skipping ropes, small balls and so on, that they use
- being able to mediate and resolve minor disputes without recourse to adults.

Of course, all of the above suggestions and ideas are only offered as stepping stones to help you formulate and implement your own active playtimes policy. You can adapt, expand, revise and improve on them in any way you see fit so that they address the particular circumstances in your own school.

KEY POINTS

- Many playground games have been forgotten or have fallen into disuse.

- All staff and children will need training on how to play games.

- The lunchtime supervisors are critical to the success of implementing an active playtimes policy.

- Gender stereotyping and negative attitudes can prevent children from taking full advantage of active playtimes.

- Playing cooperative games is an effective strategy for encouraging inclusion.

- Teachers can support the implementation of the active playtimes policy by teaching playground games in PE lessons.

- Appointing and training children to be play leaders is a good way of encouraging social inclusion as well as boosting children's self-esteem and their communication, conflict resolution and leadership skills.

5 Other issues to consider

Although the media is full of stories about the need for society in general – and children in particular – to take more exercise, these stories normally focus on adults who spend a fortune to join a gym and then never go or children being driven to school by their parents instead of walking. What rarely gets mentioned are the opportunities offered by school playtimes for getting children (and the adults who supervise them) fit. Therefore, one key thing you'll need to do is send a letter home to all the parents and carers explaining why you're introducing an active playtimes policy.

Health and safety issues

The letter will give you the chance to explain any health and safety issues to the parents and carers, such as the advisability of sending children to school with the appropriate clothing and footwear so that they can take full advantage of the opportunities now being provided to run around and be active. If the school is installing climbing frames or similar apparatus in the playground as part of the active playtimes initiative, you'll also need to reassure the parents and carers that all necessary measures will be taken to ensure that:

- children understand how to play on the equipment safely
- impact-absorbing surfaces, such as rubber, bark chips and so on, will be used
- all play on the equipment will be properly supervised
- children will wear appropriate clothing: no scarves or tops with drawstrings or cords, for example
- equipment will be checked regularly once it is in use and old or worn equipment will be replaced.

Moreover, the letter provides the perfect opportunity for you to ask the parents and carers to contribute their own favourite childhood games to the school's 'Active Playtimes Games Collection'. Indeed, some of them may well volunteer to come into the school to teach them to you and the children!

Organisational issues

It's all very well getting the staff and parents excited and enthusiastic about the idea of active playtimes, but the most important people to involve are the children. They must understand why you are making these changes to the way playtimes are used; what being active at playtimes means; how the playtimes will be organised; what you expect from them; and what they can expect from active playtimes. This can be done in several ways, such as through assemblies, circle time, school council sessions and so on. However, it is vital that the children realise that the supervisors and the play leaders will have the full backing of the teaching staff when they initiate the games and activities.

Educational issues

Given the pressure on the curriculum, using playtimes to raise children's awareness of health and fitness makes perfect sense. To give just one example, if you wanted to help the children recognise the short-term effects of exercise on the body, you could get a group of children to record their pulse rate at the start of playtime and then again at the end of playtime after they have been involved in playing a vigorous game. Ask them what they notice has happened to their pulse rates as well as about any other changes to their bodies. For example, are they out of breath? Are they sweating? If so, why?

Assessing the contribution of active playtimes to the curriculum

You can use the chart shown in figure 5.1 as a means of assessing the contribution active playtimes are making to the understanding and promotion of health and fitness issues in your school.

FIGURE 5.1 ASSESSING THE CONTRIBUTION OF ACTIVE PLAYTIMES TO THE CURRICULUM		
Subject areas	**Relevant National Curriculum statements**	**Evidence of how active playtimes are contributing to the children's understanding of each of these statements**
PSHE	What makes a healthy lifestyle; the benefits of exercise.	
PE	Pupils should be taught: about the changes that occur to their bodies as they exercise; to recognise the short-term effects of exercise on the body (KS1). Pupils should find solutions to the various challenges they encounter; they should sustain energetic activity over appropriate periods of time; they should understand what is happening to their bodies during exercise (KS2). All pupils should be taught: to warm up for and recover from exercise; about the safety risks of wearing inappropriate clothing; to engage in activities that develop cardiovascular health, flexibility, muscular strength and endurance.	
Science	**Humans as organisms (KS1)** Pupils should be taught: that taking exercise helps keep humans healthy. **Humans as organisms (KS2)** Pupils should be taught: that the heart acts as a pump; that blood circulates through arteries and veins; that exercise and rest have an effect on the pulse rate; that humans have skeletons and muscles to support and protect bodies and to help them to move.	

Active Playtimes: Key Stage 1+2 © Roger Hurn 2006, A & C Black Publishers Ltd

KEY POINTS

- It is vital to let parents and carers know about the active playtimes policy.

- Parents and carers can be a good source for providing playground games.

- Health and safety issues, such as the need for the children to wear appropriate clothing and footwear while playing, and for all playground equipment to be well maintained, must be taken into account when launching the policy.

- The children need to be clear about how active playtimes will be organised and about the roles of the supervisors and play leaders.

- You can use active playtimes to promote and assess children's understanding of health and fitness issues.

PART 2

The games

6 Warming up, cooling down and stretching games

Although it sometimes seems as if children are made of elastic and can bounce back from the type of falls and tumbles that would have an adult heading for the nearest A & E department, warming up, cooling down and stretching are as important for children as they are for any professional athlete. This is because children's bodies are still growing. Their injuries do heal more quickly than those sustained by adults, but bone and ligament injuries never heal as fully as healthy new tissue. Therefore, it's important never to just launch into vigorous games without first stretching and warming up. Moreover, when leading the stretching session remind the children not to hold their breath but to breathe normally and to stretch slowly and evenly, as quick or bouncing stretches can pull muscles and strain joints.

Of course, on the playground the children won't always have an adult around to check that they're properly warmed up before they start playing. And, naturally enough, children won't want the bother of going through an elaborate and dull series of stretches; they'll want to get straight into playing games. The trick is to make the stretching, warming up and cooling down sessions as enjoyable as possible so that they'll regard them as an essential part of the fun. The ideas for stretches, warm-ups and cool-downs provided in this chapter are designed to do just that and, because each of the stretching exercises has its own built-in playground chant, children will play them without even realising that they're doing an exercise routine. The children should always warm up their muscles before doing any stretching, so the warm up games provided here are designed to raise their heart rates and get them breathing more deeply.

6 Warming up games

Traffic lights

Age
4–7

Resources
None.

How to play
Tell the children that the command 'red' means stop, the command 'amber' means walk and the command 'green' means run. The children move around the playground in response to the commands.

This game can be made more challenging by changing the command 'amber' to mean moving on hands and feet, for example.

Corner to corner

Age
4–11

Resources
None (although plastic cones could be used to mark out four corners if the playground is too large).

How to play
Put the children into groups of five. Send one child from each group to a corner of the playground, but keep two from each group in the first corner. On your signal, one child from each group walks to tag their teammate in the next corner. As soon as they have been tagged, that person walks to the next corner and so on. The game continues until the fifth child tags the first child, who begins the next round by jogging slowly. With each new round the children increase their speed slightly, going from a walk to a slow jog, to a faster jog, to skipping, to galloping.

Remind the children to move safely and to avoid colliding with each other in the corners. While waiting for their turn, the children can run on the spot, do wall press-ups, a wall-sit, roll their shoulders, hips and ankles or do gentle stretches.

To adapt this into a cooling down game, reverse the sequence so that the first lap is at a gallop and the last lap is at walking pace.

Active Playtimes: Key Stage 1+2 © Roger Hurn 2006, A & C Black Publishers Ltd

Mirror Me

Age
4–11

Resources
None.

How to play
Put the children in pairs. One child is A, the other B. The children in each pair stand facing each other a metre apart. They must not move from the spot. The game begins when child A performs a simple movement, such as an arm raise, neck roll, running on the spot, bouncing on the spot, star jumps and so on. Child B mirrors the movement. Then child A does another movement, child B copies it and so on until the first child has completed four different types of movement and child B has copied them all. Then child B takes over and leads.

You can make this game more difficult by not allowing child B to repeat any of the moves made by child A. When child B has completed four original moves the leadership passes back to child A, and so on.

The Crown Jewels

Age
4–11

Resources
Small, shiny non-valuable objects; 'Crown Jewels' box.

How to play
Hide 'the Crown Jewels' (some small, shiny objects – plasticine wrapped in kitchen foil will do) around the playground. Tell the children they've been stolen and hidden by a magpie – a bird that can't resist bright glittery objects. The children's task is to find the jewels as quickly as possible. Each child may bring back only one 'jewel' at a time to the Crown Jewels box. Give the children a time limit. This activity can be repeated and the group can try to beat their record by collecting all of the jewels in an even faster time.

Tails you lose

Age
4–11

Resources
Coloured PE bands or ribbons.

How to play
Have half of the children attach PE bands or ribbons so they hang down from the back of their trousers or skirt like a tail, then send them to stand on one side of the playground. On your signal, the rest of the children have to chase them and try to capture their tails. If a child loses his/her tail, he/she is not out of the game but can try to capture others from children who are still wearing theirs. No child can take a tail that has already been captured. The winner is the child who has captured the most tails at the end of the game.

If you are playing this game with a mixed age group, remind the older children to take care not to knock the younger ones over.

Leader of the gang

Age
7–11

Resources
None.

How to play
Put the children in a circle with one child in the centre. This child is the 'Detective' and his/her job is to arrest the 'Leader of the Gang'. The 'Detective' must close his/her eyes while one child in the circle is chosen to be the 'Leader of the Gang', who will lead the children in a range of fitness activities such as jogging on the spot, star jumps, knee lifts and so on. The Leader should be encouraged to choose activities that move large muscles and get the heart rate up; teachers should suggest activities to the children that are appropriate for their age, level and ability. The group then follows the Leader, doing whatever fitness activity he/she does. The Detective is asked to open his/her eyes and try to guess the identity of the Leader. The Leader changes activity every 10 seconds; the group follows the Leader, but doesn't look directly at him/her. The Detective has three chances to spot who the Leader is. If correct, he/she 'arrests' the Leader, who takes over as Detective in the centre of the circle and a new Leader is chosen. However, if he/she runs out of guesses, he/she changes place with the Leader and the game restarts with a new 'Leader of the Gang'.

Hop, skip and jump

Age
7–11

Resources
None.

How to play
The children have to travel around the playground by hopping, skipping and jumping. They change their mode of travelling on the shouted commands:
'Hop!' 'Skip!' 'Jump!'

Hearts, Clubs, Diamonds, Spades

Age
7–11

Resources
A scarf.

How to play
Name each corner of the playground after a suit of cards: Hearts, Clubs, Diamonds, Spades. Then blindfold one child and tell the others to run and stand in any of the four corners. When they are all standing in a corner of their choice, the blindfolded child calls out the name of one of the suits. All the children who are in that corner are out of the game. The children who are left now have 30 seconds to change corners. The blindfolded child then calls out the name of a corner (the child should not call out the names in any particular order and can repeat a name if they so wish) and the children who have chosen that corner are eliminated. The game continues until there is only one child left. That child now becomes the caller.

Crab racing

Age
7–11

Resources
Chalk.

How to play
Draw two straight lines 10 metres apart on the playground. One line is the starting line, the other is the finishing line. Ask the children to lie on their backs next to each other with their feet behind the starting line. Then tell them to make themselves into crabs by pushing themselves up so they are balancing on their hands and feet with their backs arched upwards. On the word 'Go!' they scuttle like crabs to the finishing line.

Cooling down games

It's bedtime

Age
4–7

Resources
None.

How to play:
The children start off by walking around the playground. When the leader calls out 'It's bedtime!' the children have to mime getting ready for bed, using lots of exaggerated actions and stretches. The game ends when all the children are 'asleep' with their heads lolling on their chests.

Moon-walking

Age
4–11

Resources
None.

How to play
The children move around an area at a steady pace. On your command they move in a directed style, for example like an astronaut on the moon, a person with their feet stuck in treacle, running in slow motion, sliding like graceful ice skaters and so on.

Let's do it!

Age
4–11

Resources
None.

How to play
The children have to respond very enthusiastically by shouting 'Let's do it!' to every suggestion the leader calls out. For example, the leader shouts 'Touch your nose!' and the children shout 'Let's do it!' and touch their noses. Then the leader calls out a succession of cooling down actions for the children to do, for example neck rolls, touching their toes, reaching for the sky and so on. They comply and shout 'Let's do it!' each time. The game finishes when the leader says 'Let's close our eyes and breathe slowly and deeply while I count to ten'.

Changing the guard

Age
4–11

Resources
None.

How to play
The children march up and down on the spot. One person acts as the sergeant-major and gives the orders, for example 'Quick march' 'Right turn' 'Left turn' 'Attention'.

I, Robot.

Age
4–11

Resources
None.

How to play
The children pretend to be robots. On the command 'Go!' they walk about like robots but, as their batteries begin to run down, they move more and more slowly until they finally grind to a halt.

Chasing your own tail

Age
4–11

Resources
None.

How to play
The children make a snake by standing in a line, each holding the hips of the child in front of them. The child at the head of the snake then tries to catch the child at the tail end.

Stretching games
Sky, ground, turn around

Age
4–7

Resources
None.

How to play
This is a very gentle stretching exercise for the arms, shoulders, back and legs. The children face the leader, who chants 'Let's stretch so high we'll touch the sky'. The children respond 'We'll stretch so high we'll touch the sky', then slowly stretch their arms up above their heads until they are fully extended. Then the leader says 'Let's sink right down 'til we touch the ground'. The children reply 'We'll sink right down 'til we touch the ground' and lower themselves slowly into a crouching position with their fingertips touching the ground. The leader says 'Up from the ground and slowly turn around' and the children reply 'We're up from the ground and turning around'. They slowly stand upright with their arms stretched out horizontally as far as they will go and turn around in a full circle.

The elephant stomp

Age
4–7

Resources
None.

How to play
The elephant stomp stretches the shoulders and arms and strengthens the legs. The children put their hands together and bend forwards slowly from an upright position until their chests are horizontal to the ground. They then stomp along, swinging their arms like elephants' trunks and chanting:

'We are elephants having a romp
We're all doing the elephant stomp
If you see us coming, get out of the way
'Cos we're doing the elephant stomp today.'

6

Grizzly bears on the prowl

Age
4–7

Resources
None.

How to play
This game stretches and strengthens the back, stomach and hamstrings. Have the children
walk on all fours while chanting:
'We are great big grizzly bears
If you see us coming, you'd better beware
We're strong and fierce and love to growl
'Cos we're grizzly bears on the prowl.'

The children must keep as low as possible with their knees and chest off the ground. One
child leads the prowl and gives the commands 'Forward! Back! Sideways!' to change direction
at the end of the chant, which is then repeated to accompany the movement.

Fly like Superman

Age
4–11

Resources
None.

How to play
This game stretches and strengthens the back, shoulder, arms, bottom and hamstrings. The
children take up a position whereby their hands and feet are flat on the ground, shoulder
width apart. Their bodies should be making the shape of an upside down V. Then they chant:
'I am Superman and I'm going to fly
Watch me soar up to the sky.'

Next, they walk their hands forwards until their stomachs are about 10 centimetres above the
ground. They should now look like
Superman flying through the air. They
hold the position while they chant:
'I am Superman and I dare
To fly like a bird right through the air.'

Then they walk on their hands back to
the starting position, chanting:
'I am Superman as you can see
I bet you wish you could fly like me.'

Active Playtimes: Key Stage 1+2 © Roger Hurn 2006, A & C Black Publishers Ltd

Flamingo

Age
4–11

Resources
None.

How to play
This game stretches the thigh muscles (quadriceps). The children chant:
'A flamingo is a bird to see
It can stand on one leg just like me.'

While chanting this, they keep one leg straight and bend the other one up behind them. They do this by reaching down and holding their ankle from behind, then very gently pull their leg up until their heel touches their bottom. Then they change legs and repeat the chant.

Games from around the world

The sly fox

Age
4–7

Country of origin
Greece

Resources
None.

How to play
One child stands with their back to the others, who stand about 10 metres away. The child with their back to the others chants:
'I am the sly fox and I never sleep. Beware all of you who up on me creep!'

While the sly fox is chanting, the other children move towards him/her. At the end of the chant the sly fox spins around and tries to catch someone moving. If the sly fox is unable to do so, he/she can walk among the children and, without touching them, try to make them smile or laugh. If the sly fox succeeds, the child who smiled or laughed takes the sly fox's place for the next game.

Bear tag

Age
4–7

Country of origin
Canada

Resources
None.

How to play
Choose two children to be 'it'. These two have to try to tag the other players. None of the children are allowed to run – they must speed-walk. When a child is tagged, he/she has to drop down on all fours and walk along, growling like a bear. However, if he/she meets up with another bear and they shake paws, they can both stand upright and join back in with the game of tag.

Active Playtimes: Key Stage 1+2 © Roger Hurn 2006, A & C Black Publishers Ltd

Signor Lupo, che ora è?
(What's the time, Mr Wolf?)

Age
4–7

Country of origin
Italy

Resources
Chalk.

How to play

Choose one child to be Mr Wolf. Mr Wolf stands with his back to the other children, who wait behind a chalk line about 10 metres away. The children call out 'What's the time, Mr Wolf?' (or 'Signor Lupo, che ora è?') Mr Wolf doesn't turn around but growls out an answer, for example 'It's six o'clock.' The children then walk six paces towards the wolf. They ask him again and he gives a different time, and the children take the same number of steps towards the wolf as the time he gives, so 'Three o'clock' equals three steps. When Mr Wolf thinks they're close enough, he finally roars out 'It's dinner time!' The children scatter and Mr Wolf tries to catch them. The child who is caught then takes over as Mr Wolf and the game starts all over again.

Catch the chicks

Age
4–8

Country of origin
Taiwan

Resources
Chalk or cones.

How to play

Mark out an 'eagle's nest' using the chalk or cones. Choose one child to be an eagle and one to be a hen (or a cockerel). The rest of the children are chicks and stand in a row behind the hen. It is the hen's job to protect the chicks from the eagle. The eagle tries to catch the chicks, and puts each captured chick in its 'nest'. The eagle wins if it catches all the chicks within a certain time. The last chick to be caught takes the eagle's place. If the hen wins (that is if the eagle doesn't catch all the chicks within the time limit), he/she becomes the eagle.

Chicken's got the measles

Age
4–11

Country of origin
Ireland

Resources
None

How to play
The children stand in a circle with their legs apart. The children sing the following rhyme:
'Chicken's got the measles, the measles, the measles
Chicken's got the measles, inside out.'

The children jump from legs crossed (right leg in front) to legs apart to legs crossed (left leg in front) along with the rhyme, and whoever has their legs uncrossed at the end of the rhyme has to leave the circle. This continues until only one child is left.

French cricket

Age
4–11

Country of origin
England

Resources
A cricket bat; a soft ball.

How to play
One child is the batter, all the other children are fielders. The fielders bowl the ball underarm at the batter, trying to hit either the batter's feet or legs. If they manage to do so, the child who bowled the ball takes over as the batter. If the batter knocks the ball up into the air and one of the fielders catches it, that fielder becomes the batter. The children can feint to bowl and then quickly throw the ball to another fielder, who tries to hit the batter's legs before he or she can block it with the bat. The batter can't move his/her feet, but can use the bat to protect his/her legs. The fielders bowl the ball from wherever the batter knocked it. The trick is to bowl from behind the batter.

Hopscotch

Age
4–11

Country of origin
Roman Britain

Resources
Chalk; markers.

How to play
Mark a hopscotch grid with numbered sections. Each player has a marker, for example a bottle top or button. The first player

stands behind the starting line and throws his/her marker into square one. The marker must land completely inside the square, otherwise the player loses his/her turn. The player hops over square one into square two and continues to hop to the end of the court. If the court has squares that are side by side the player can straddle them with the left foot landing in the left square and the right foot landing in the right square, but single squares must be hopped in with only one foot. For the first single square either foot can be used. When the player reaches the end of the grid, he/she turns around and hops back again. The player must pick up the marker without losing his/her balance or stepping on a line, then hop out of the grid and continue the game by tossing the stone into square two and so on. Once a player has completed all the numbers in the grid, he/she may write his/her initials in any square of his/her choice, and then only he/she may step in it: the other players will have to hop or jump over it. A player is out if he/she puts two feet down in a single square, steps on a line, puts his/her hand on the ground or goes into a square containing someone else's initials.

Sometimes a semi-circular 'rest area' is added onto one end of the hopscotch court where the player can rest for a moment before hopping back. Some courts also have squares marked 'safe' or 'home'. The players can hop through these in any way they want.

7

The cat and the rat

Age
4–11

Country of origin
Democratic Republic of Congo

Resources
None.

How to play
The children line up in four equal rows, leaving a corridor between each one – the rows of children should be in touching distance of each other. The children in each row hold hands. One child is picked to be the caller, one to be the rat and another to be the cat. A time limit is set. The rat runs up and down the corridors with the cat chasing it. When the caller shouts 'Stop that rat!' the players in the rows stop holding hands with each other and instead join hands with the children in the row across from them. This changes the direction of the corridors and the rat must adapt to the change or be trapped. The caller should change the direction of the rows quite frequently. The game ends when the rat has been caught or the time limit has been reached. Then the children who've been the caller, the rat and the cat choose other children to take on their roles for the next game.

Lion! Lion! (Mbube! Mbube!)

Age
4–11

Country of origin
South Africa

Resources
Two scarves.

How to play
The children stand in a circle. Two children stand in the middle of the circle: one is a lion and one is an impala. Use the scarves to blindfold these two children, then spin each one around three times. The lion then has to hunt the impala. The children in the circle give guidance to the lion and the impala as to where each other is by the way they chant. If the lion is moving away from the impala, they chant 'Lion! Lion!' slowly and softly. As the lion gets closer to the impala, the chanting gets quicker and louder. (If you think it is more fun or authentic, you can use the word Zulus use for calling a lion, which is 'mbube' – pronounced 'mboo bay'.) Set a time limit for the lion to catch the impala. If the impala survives, choose a new lion to hunt the impala. If the lion catches the impala within the time limit, choose a new impala.

Here in Kikuyu

Age
4–11

Country of origin
Kenya

Resources
None.

How to play
The children form two lines facing each other. The first line steps forwards one pace and sings (to the tune of 'Here we go round the mulberry bush'):
'This is the way we chop our wood, chop our wood, chop our wood
This is the way we chop our wood, here in the land of Kikuyu.'

As they sing, they mime the action of cutting wood. When they've finished, the line steps back and the other line steps forwards, singing:
'This is the way we build our fire,
*   build our fire, build our fire*
This is the way we build our fire, here
*   in the land of Kikuyu.'*

As they sing, they stoop to lay wood and blow on an imaginary fire. The groups continue taking turns singing and miming new actions.

Ideas for actions

'This is the way we carry our water'	Balancing imaginary gourds on their heads
'This is the way we grind our corn'	Kneeling and grinding corn between two stones
'This is the way we carry the baby'	Carrying imaginary babies on their backs and rocking from side to side
'This is the way we hunt the lion'	Crouching and thrusting imaginary spears

Snake's tail

Age
4–11

Country of origin
South Africa

Resources
Cones or chalk.

How to play

Use the cones or chalk to mark out the snake's territory (don't make it too large). The children stand inside the marked space. Pick one child to be the snake. The other children must avoid being caught by the snake, who wants them for his tail. When the snake catches someone, that child has to become part of the snake's tail by joining hands with the snake. The new elongated snake now tries to catch fresh prey to make its tail even longer. Each child who is caught holds the hand of the child caught just before them. Only the child who is the snake can catch new prey, but it can use its tail to trap other players. The last child to remain free from the snake's clutches becomes the new snake.

Duck and Goose

Age
4–11

Country of origin
USA

Resources
None.

How to play

The children sit in a circle and face one another. One child is chosen to be 'it' and walks around the outside of the circle. As he/she walks he/she lightly touches each child on the top of their head and names them as either a duck or a goose. When someone is told he/she is a goose, he/she jumps up and chases after the child who is 'it'. The aim is for the 'goose' to tag the child who is 'it' before he/she can run around the circle and sit down in the goose's place. If the goose fails, he/she becomes 'it' and the game goes on. If he/she succeeds, the child who was 'it' has to go and sit in the centre of the circle. The goose then becomes 'it' and the game continues. The child in the middle can only rejoin the circle when another child is caught. The child in the middle then takes the caught child's place.

Stick in the Mud

Age
7–11

Country of origin
Scotland

Resources
None.

How to play
Divide the children into two teams. One team is doing the chasing and one team is being chased. When a child is caught, that child has to stand still with his/her legs apart and can only be freed if a teammate crawls through his/her legs. The game finishes when all the children being chased are caught, then the teams reverse the roles.

The fisher

Age
7–11

Country of origin
Wales

Resources
None.

How to play
Choose one child to be 'the Fisher' while the rest of the children split into three equal teams. In a space with four corners, each team chooses a corner and a type of fish, for example haddock. The children go and stand in their corners. The child who is the Fisher stands in the middle and shouts out the name of one type of fish. The team who have chosen that type of fish run to the empty corner and the person who is the Fisher tries to catch them by touching them. The children who are caught either go into the 'Fisher's basket' (an area of the playground where they have to stay until the end of the game) or become the Fisher's helpers and try to catch other children. The last child left becomes the Fisher for the next game.

Chegi

Age
7–11

Country of origin
Korea

Resources
Shuttlecocks.

How to play
Playing individually, each child kicks the head of the shuttlecock repeatedly to keep it up in the air. They can use one foot or both feet. The aim of the game is to see how many times they can kick the shuttlecock and keep it up in the air before it hits the ground.

Choom-choom

Age
7–11

Country of origin
USA (Cree Nation)

Resources
None.

How to play
Two teams of children line up in single file. Each child holds the waist of the person in front of them. They squat down and, chanting 'choom-choom', they shuffle forwards. The winning team is the one that can go the furthest without falling over.

Quemada (Burnt one)

Age
7–11

Country of origin
Brazil

Resources
Chalk; a soft ball.

How to play
Use the chalk to mark out a playing area that is divided into four parts, as shown below.

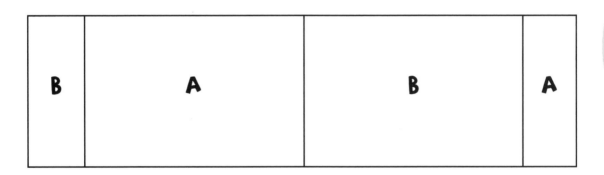

The two large areas are called 'fields', while the narrow areas are called 'cemeteries'. Split the children into two teams (A and B). The teams each go and stand in their field, but one person from each team starts in the cemetery. They are 'dead'. The child in one of the cemeteries starts the game by throwing the ball over the heads of the opposing team to their 'living' teammates on the far field. They have to catch the ball and throw it against members of the opposite team. If the ball touches a player from that team, that player is 'La Quemada' – 'the burnt one' – and is 'dead'. The 'dead' players go to the cemetery and the game finishes when everybody from one team is in the cemetery.

Parada! (Stop!)

Age
7–11

Country of origin
Colombia

Resources
A small soft ball.

How to play
Choose one child and give him/her the ball. The other children stand by that child, who throws the ball up and calls out the name of one of the other children. When the thrower does this, the rest of the children have to run as far away as possible. The named child has to stop running and dash back to try to catch the ball before it hits the ground. If the child is successful, he/she can throw the ball back up into the air, call out another name and run away. However, if the child doesn't catch the ball and it bounces, as soon as he/she has the ball in his/her hands, he/she must call out 'Parada!' ('Stop!'). All the other children have to stop running immediately. The child with the ball now takes three strides towards the nearest child and attempts to hit that child by throwing the ball at them. The thrower can only aim at the body – not the head. If the child misses, he/she restarts the game by throwing the ball up and calling out another name. However, if he/she hits the other child with the ball, that child has to restart the game.

Oonch neech (up and down)

Age
7–11

Country of origin
Pakistan

Resources
Mats, benches, climbing frames if available.

How to play
One person is 'it' and has to try to tag the other players. However, the other children cannot be tagged if their feet are off the ground, that is standing on a mat, bench, climbing frame and so on. They can only stay off the ground while they count up to 10. The tagger has to catch all the other children; the last player left is the tagger in the next game.

Lempang Tali (Slap string)

Age
7–11

Country of origin
Malaysia

Resources
A long skipping rope.

How to play
Two children hold the ends of the skipping rope and twirl it in a circular motion, either clockwise or anti-clockwise, so that it slaps against the ground. Other children take it in turns to jump over the rope as it does so. Each time they do this, the two players twirling the rope say 'Lempang Tali'. When one of the players catches the rope with their feet and stops it slapping, he/she swaps places with one of the two children who have been twirling the rope.

Anto akiyire (It wasn't put behind you)

Age
7–11

Country of origin
Ghana

Resources
A cloth.

How to play
The children sit in a circle. One of them holds a cloth and runs around the outside of the circle singing 'anto akiyire o anto akiyire o' (pronounced 'an-toh akee-year-ay'). ('It wasn't put behind you.') The children in the circle reply 'Yie yie yie!' The chant and response are repeated several times until the runner chants 'Obiba bewu o' (somebody's child is about to suffer or die) 'Yie yie yie. Kapoi poi.' The children in the circle respond by chanting: 'Yie yie yie.' None of the children must look at the runner at any time. Then the runner drops the cloth behind one of the children in the circle, who has to grab the cloth, leap up and give chase. He/she must catch the runner before the runner can complete the circuit three times and sit down in the vacant place. If he/she catches the runner, he/she gives the cloth back to the runner and the game restarts. If he/she doesn't catch the runner, he/she takes the runner's place.

Down! Down! Down!

Age
7–11

Country of origin
Australia

Resources
A tennis ball.

How to play
The children throw a tennis ball to each other. When someone drops the ball, the others shout 'Down on one knee' and the child who dropped the ball goes down on one knee. If he/she drops it again, everyone chants: 'Down on two knees'. If he/she drops it a third time, everyone chants 'Down on one elbow', and if he/she drops it a fourth time the chant is 'Down on both elbows'. If he/she misses the ball again, the chant is 'Down on your chin' and the child has no more chances after that. However, each time he/she manages to catch the ball, he/she can move back up one position.

8 Non-competitive games

Amoebas

Age
4–11

Resources
Cones.

How to play
A circle of five children face outwards and, with their arms linked, try to move as one around a series of cones.

Shake-a-hand!

Age
4–11

Resources
None.

How to play
Everyone dances while the leader claps his/her hands rhythmically. The leader then stops clapping and calls out instructions telling the players to get into groups. The make-up of these groups can be decided any number of ways, for example by hair colour, by number and so on. Then, on the shout of 'Shake-a-hand!' everyone in the group shakes hands.

Beanbag bagged

Age
4–11

Resources
A beanbag and a carrier bag.

How to play
The children sit in a circle. One child stands in the centre of a circle holding a carrier bag so that it is wide open. The children have to pass a beanbag right around the circle using only their feet. If they drop it, the bag goes back to the start. When the beanbag has been right around the circle, the last child has to balance the bag on his/her foot and flick it up in the air so that the child in the centre of the circle can catch it in the carrier bag.

8

Pass it on

Age
4–11

Resources
A beanbag.

How to play
The children stand in a line. The first child has a beanbag tucked under his/her chin. The children must pass the beanbag from one end of the line to the other without dropping it. If they drop the bag, they must begin again. At no time may the children use their hands to pass the beanbag on.

It takes two

Age
4–11

Resources
None.

How to play
Put the children into pairs. Choose one child to be the leader and one to be the follower. The leader tells the follower to do a particular action, for example two press-ups. When the supervisor/play leader calls 'Switch!' they switch roles. The children keep switching roles, but in the second round the leaders can't talk and must demonstrate what they want the follower to do. In the third round, the leaders can't talk and must have their hands behind their backs.

Active Playtimes: Key Stage 1+2 © Roger Hurn 2006, A & C Black Publishers Ltd

Monster! Monster!

Age
4–11

Resources
A ball.

How to play
One child is selected to be the 'Monster'. This child takes the ball and stands with his/her back to the rest of the children. The Monster throws the ball backwards over his/her head. If someone catches the ball, the Monster is out and the child who caught the ball takes the Monster's place. If no-one catches the ball, one child picks up the ball and hides it behind his/her back. All the children now put their arms behind their backs, then chant:

'Monster! Monster! Big and tall,
Won't you tell us who's got the ball?'

The Monster then turns around and tries to guess. He/she points to one child and roars,
'Monster, Monster is no fool.
Monster says you've got the ball.'

The game continues until the Monster guesses correctly and swaps places with the child who was hiding the ball.

9 Chasing games

Chain reaction

Age
4–11

Resources
None.

How to play
The children pair up with each other by holding hands or linking arms and scatter around the playground. One child is chosen to be 'it' and chases after the pairs. When a pair is caught, they split up and become chasers. The game ends when there are no pairs left.

Red lion

Age
4–11

Resources
Chalk or four cones.

How to play
Mark out a lion's 'den' using the chalk or cones. One child is chosen to be the 'Red Lion' and goes into the den. The other children chant:
'Red lion, Red lion, come out of your den
Whoever you catch will be one of your men.'

The lion then chases after the other children. When the lion catches someone, he/she takes that person back to the den. The chant begins again and the two lions come racing out together to try to catch someone. The game continues in this way until all the children have been caught. The last child to be caught is the new 'Red Lion'.

 Active Playtimes: Key Stage 1+2 © Roger Hurn 2006, A & C Black Publishers Ltd

Pirate Island

Age
4–11

Resources
Chalk or cones.

How to play
Mark out an area of the playground to be 'Pirate Island'. Mark two or three other small areas to be 'safe harbours'. Pick four of the children to be pirates. The others are sailors. The pirates go to Pirate Island and the sailors go to a safe harbour. On the cry 'Set sail!' the sailors must leave the safe harbours. The pirates chase after them and try to capture them by tagging them. The sailors cannot return to the safe harbour they have just left, but must go to a new one. The regulator of the game calls 'Set sail' at regular intervals to stop sailors from spending too long resting in the safe harbours. As and when the sailors are captured, they are taken to Pirate Island. To free them, other sailors must run up to the Island and tag them. The game continues until all the sailors have been captured. The last four to be captured become the new pirate crew.

Link up

Age
4–11

Resources
None.

How to play
Choose one child to be 'it' and another to be the runner. Put the rest of the children in pairs. Each child links arms with his/her partner. The pairs then spread out around the playground. The child who is 'it' chases the runner. The runner tries to link arms with one of the children in one of the pairs. When this happens, the other child in that pair spins away and becomes the new runner. If the child who is 'it' catches the runner they reverse roles. No immediate tagging-back is allowed.

9

The Freezers are coming!

Age
4–11

Resources
Red bibs or PE bands; blue bibs or PE bands.

How to play
Set the scene by telling the children that the 'Freezers' are from outer space and they've come to turn all humans into icicles by tagging them. However, explain that humans who have been turned into icicles can be saved by another group of space aliens called the 'Melters', who can unfreeze human icicles by touching them on the shoulder. Once unfrozen, the humans have to 'melt' into the ground before they can jump up and run away. 'Freezers' can't catch 'Melters' or vice versa. Put the children into three groups. One group will be the 'Freezers', one large group will be the humans and one much smaller group will be the 'Melters'. The 'Freezers' will wear the blue bibs while the 'Melters' will wear the red bibs. Set a time limit for the 'Freezers' to turn all the humans into icicles.

Diamond smugglers

Age
4–11

Resources
A clear plastic bead small enough to be hidden in a child's hand.

How to play
Put the children into two teams. One team will be the customs officers while the other team will be the smugglers. There should be fewer customs officers than smugglers. The teams go to opposite ends of the playground. The smugglers go into a huddle; one of them takes the 'diamond' and holds it in his/her hand so it can't be seen. Then, on a given signal, the smugglers all run across the playground to the other side. Each one tries to fool the customs officers by pretending to have the 'diamond'. The customs officers try to catch them. If caught, the smugglers have to open their hands to show they're not smuggling anything. The smugglers win if the child carrying the 'diamond' can get to the other side of the playground without being caught.

10

Skipping games

Rock-a-bye baby

Age
4–7

Resources
A skipping rope.

How to play
Two children swing the skipping rope from side to side as if they were rocking a baby in a cradle. The other children take turns to jump over it.

Teddy bear, teddy bear

Age
4–7

Resources
A long skipping rope.

How to play
Two children turn a rope and one child skips in the middle to the chant of:
'Teddy bear, teddy bear, turn around
Teddy bear, teddy bear, touch the ground
Teddy bear, teddy bear, climb the stairs
Teddy bear, teddy bear, say your prayers
Teddy bear, teddy bear, switch off the light
Teddy bear, teddy bear, say goodnight.'

The child who is skipping mimes the actions. If the skipper trips over the rope, another child takes over and the chant begins again.

Snakes alive!

Age
4–11

Resources
Skipping ropes.

How to play
Put the children into pairs and give each pair a skipping rope. One child holds one end of the rope, squats down and makes it slither like a snake while the other child tries to jump on the rope. If the jumper is successful, the children swap roles.

Two little dickie birds

Age
4–11

Resources
A skipping rope.

How to play
Two children, one at each end, hold the rope and turn it. As they do so, everyone chants:

'Two little dickie birds, sitting on the wall — (two children start to jump over the rope)

One named Peter, one named Paul — (the children wave at the sound of their name)

Fly away Peter, fly away Paul — (the children jump out as their name is called)

Don't come back 'til your birthday's called

January, February … December — (the children jump back in when their birthday month is called)

Now fly away, fly away, fly away all.' — (the two children jump out).

10 Salt and pepper

Age
7–11

Resources
A long skipping rope.

How to play
One child spins around holding one end of the rope. The other children have to jump over the rope as it revolves past them. As they jump they have to chant 'salt, mustard, vinegar, pepper'. Every time they say the word 'pepper', the child holding the rope spins it more quickly. Anyone who fails to jump over the rope is out. The last child left jumping is the winner and spins the rope around in the next game.

Jumping Jack

Age
7–11

Resources
A long skipping rope.

How to play
Two children twirl the rope in a circular motion and another child starts to jump over the rope. The children who are twirling the rope chant the rhyme and the child who is jumping has to mime the actions described:

'Jumping Jack, Jumping Jack, hitch a ride
(Jumping Jack has to pretend to flag down a car with his/her thumb)

Jumping Jack, Jumping Jack, hold your sides
(Jumping Jack presses his/her arms against his/her sides)

Jumping Jack, Jumping Jack, touch your toes
(Jumping Jack touches his/her toes as he/she skips)

Jumping Jack, Jumping Jack, let's see you start to doze
(Jumping Jack presses his/her hands together and puts them to the side of his/her head, as if sleeping)

Jumping Jack, Jumping Jack, put on your mac
(Jumping Jack mimes putting on a coat)

Jumping Jack, Jumping Jack, jump right out and don't come back!'
(Jumping Jack says 'I'll be back' as he/she skips out of the rope)

Then the next Jumping Jack takes over and the chant begins again.

Double bounce

Age
7–11

Resources
A skipping rope.

How to play
Two children swing the rope and another child jumps over it in a sequence made up and called by one of the children holding the rope, for example: 'Bounce, bounce, right hop, left hop, left hop, bounce' and so on. The sequence continues until the child jumping the rope either catches the rope with his/her foot or misses the command.

11 Ball games

Boss ball

Age
4–11

Resources
A soft ball.

How to play
This game needs to be played in a fairly large area (around 400 square metres). Choose one child to be 'Boss'. This child has to chase after the other children and throw the ball so it hits one of the others on their legs. Once the Boss has done this, the child hit by the ball also becomes a Boss. From this point on, no Boss can run when they have the ball. Instead, they have to work as a team by passing the ball to each other. The children who are being chased can fend the ball off by knocking it away with their fists. However, if the Boss catches the ball before it bounces, that child is out and becomes another Boss. The last child left becomes the new Boss and the game restarts.

Donkey drop

Age
4–11

Resources
A small ball.

How to play
Two children throw a ball to each other. The first time a child drops the ball, he/she must say the letter 'd'. The next time he/she drops it, he/she must say the letters 'd' and 'o', and so on. The game continues until one child spells out the complete word 'donkey'.

Active Playtimes: Key Stage 1+2 © Roger Hurn 2006, A & C Black Publishers Ltd

Piggy in the middle

Age
4–11

Resources
A small ball.

How to play
Two children throw a ball to each other while a third child, 'piggy in the middle', tries to intercept it. If 'piggy' manages to catch the ball, he/she changes place with the child who threw the ball.

Double-ball

Age
4–11

Resources
A wall; tennis balls.

How to play
Each child bounces two tennis balls off the wall one after the other and catches them while chanting a rhyme. They can throw the balls in many different ways, for example underhand ('under'), overhand ('over'), underhand throw against the wall so it bounces off the floor before being caught ('raindrop'), throwing the ball at the ground so that it bounces up onto the wall and back to the thrower ('bouncy'). The child throws the ball at the end of each line of the rhyme. If the child misses a catch or makes a throw that doesn't correspond to the action, for example throws a 'bouncy' instead of a 'raindrop', the next child takes over. If the child completes the sequence, he/she continues but this time uses only one hand. If he/she manages this, he/she repeats the sequence using the other hand.
There are any number of rhymes children can use to play this game. Here is one:

'Wayne Rooney can't score goals
He eats way too many sausage rolls.
I don't know but it's been said
Owen's boots are made of lead
I don't know but I've been told
Beckham's boots are made of gold' (and so on).

Slalom relay

Age
4–11

Resources
Two footballs; chalk; some plastic cones.

How to play
Put the children into two teams. Have them line up side by side behind a chalk line – there should be a gap of about three metres between the two teams. The two teams should then sit down. Put the cones – about a metre apart from each other – in two rows, one row in front of each team. Give the first child in each team a football. On a given signal, the child with the ball has to stand up and dribble the ball slalom-style between the cones and back, then the next child in the team takes over. The children cannot take over the ball until it has crossed the chalk line. If a player misses out one of the cones, he/she must go back and go around it. The first team to complete the slalom course and sit down one behind the other with the first player holding the ball on his/her lap is the winner.

The game can be made more varied by changing the way the players travel with the ball around the cones, for example the ball can be:

- bounced basketball-style
- carried underarm rugby-style
- held between the knees
- repeatedly thrown up and caught.

Wall ball

Age
7–11

Resources
A wall; two cones; a soft ball; some chalk.

How to play
Mark a line with chalk a few metres away from the wall. Place two cones five metres apart against the wall. A small group of children stand up against the wall between the two cones. Another child takes the ball and stands behind the chalk line. He/she must throw the ball and try to hit the other children below the knee with the ball. These children must try to dodge the ball. When a child is hit, he/she changes places with the thrower.

Foot squash

Age
7–11

Resources
A wall space; a small ball; chalk.

How to play
Mark out a goal on a wall using chalk. The children take it in turns to kick a small ball against the goal. They are only allowed to kick the ball once per round. The ball must hit the wall within the space marked for the goal. If they miss the goal or take more than one touch of the ball, they are out. The game continues until only one child is left.

Hand squash

Age
7–11

Resources
A wall space; a small ball; chalk.

How to play
This game is played in exactly the same way as 'Foot squash' (see above), but the children use their hands instead of their feet.

Seven-up

Age
7–11

Resources
A wall; a small ball.

How to play
The children stand about two metres away from a wall. They throw the ball at the wall and call out a number. Each number has a different action to go with it, for example:

- 'One'   throw the ball at the wall and catch it
- 'Two'   let the ball bounce before catching it (do this move twice)
- 'Three'   clap hands before catching it (do this move three times)
- 'Four'   turn around and catch the ball before it bounces (do this move four times)
- 'Five'   do a double hand-clap behind the back before catching the ball (do this move five times)
- 'Six'   squat down and touch the ground before catching the ball (do this move six times)
- 'Seven'   clap hands once in front of the body and once behind the back before catching the ball (do this move seven times)

Bucket ball

Age
7–11

Resources
Two buckets or wastepaper bins;
chalk; a small ball.

How to play
Use the chalk to mark out two
circles on the ground about
20 metres apart. Make each
one large enough for a child holding

a bucket to stand inside. Divide the children into two teams,
A and B. One child from each team takes a bucket and goes to stand inside one of the circles. The
rest of team A stand in front of team B's bucket holder and vice versa. No member of either team,
apart from the bucket holders, is allowed inside the circles. The two teams turn and face each
other. Two children, one from each team, stand back to back at a spot halfway between the two
bucket areas. The referee throws a ball straight up above their heads. They jump up and each tries
to knock the ball back towards their own team. The object of the game is for a team to try to
throw the ball into the bucket held by their own player. Players can throw the ball to each other,
but they are not allowed to run with it. They can try to intercept the other team's passes, but
must not knock the ball out of their hands. The first team to score five 'buckets' is the winner.

Skittle ball

Age
7–11

Resources
Chalk; two skittles; a small ball.

How to play
Skittle ball is played in the same way as bucket ball, except that the object of the game is for
one team to knock over the other team's skittle. No child is allowed inside the circle
containing the skittle. The players protect their own skittle using their hands and legs.

Bibliography

Blatchford, P. (1998), *Social Life in School: Pupils' experiences of breaktime and recess from 6 to 16*, Routledge Falmer, London

Spock, B. (2005), *Dr. Spock's Baby and Child Care*, Simon & Schuster, London

Index

Notes

Notes

Notes

Notes